Cardinal Marks

poems by

Virginia LeBaron

Finishing Line Press
Georgetown, Kentucky

Cardinal Marks

ACKNOWLEDGMENTS

In gratitude to the teachers and mentors who encouraged me to keep
writing.

Publisher: Leah Huete de Maines
Editor: Christen Kincaid
Cover Art: Hope Davis
Author Photo: Jen Fariello Photography
Cover Design: Elizabeth Maines McCleavy

Printed in the USA on acid-free paper.
Order online: www.finishinglinepress.com
              also available on amazon.com

Author inquiries and mail orders:
Finishing Line Press
P. O. Box 1626
Georgetown, Kentucky 40324
U. S. A.

Table of Contents

North 1

Where I need my mother to stand 2
Those Bound to Earth 3
Ocean City, New Jersey 4
Unseen 5
Sprinklers 7
Milton 8
Rape 9

South.. 10

Mia's room 11
Nest. 13
Packing Out 15
Weight 17
Borders 18
Patio 803 19
Father's Day 20

East... 21

Epiphyte 22
Alopecia 23
The Old Artist and the Apprentice 24
Explaining the Clover (again) 25

West.. 26

Tucson 27
Catharsis 28
Clear Margins 29
Antaeus, 1994 31
Poia Lake 33

Cardinal marks: sea marks (buoys or other floating or fixed structures) indicating danger and the direction of the safest water with reference to the four main points of the compass, North, South, East and West.

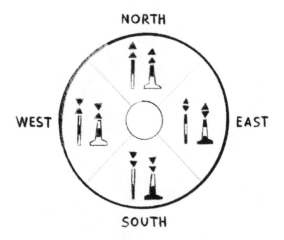

North

Where I need my mother to stand

I imagine her
the last night
of his life

That last sad night
when he could no longer stand
lying in dampness
in the bed they shared for 34 years
with the white cotton quilt
and my mother, worn
whispering
we have to wait
until the nurses come
I cannot move you

In a flannel nightgown
and thick glasses
Her coarse dark hair wild
hands pale, papery
smelling vaguely like vinegar

I see her pat baby powder
on his arms and swollen legs
in soft, slow circles
kiss his pale, frightened face
keep watch on the past
that steps out of the shadows
and convenes
at the foot of the bed

The tender, liminal place
that is neither light, nor dark
but the dusky in-between

the snow
before footsteps
fall

Those Bound to Earth

Sister Ford is dying today.
All the doctors
in their stiff white
jackets and all the nurses
in green scrubs
agree. It is my turn
to give her a bath.
Her breathing erratic
like trains shuddering
down long forked tracks
and grinding to stops.
This too has a name:
Cheyne-Stokes res-pi-
ra-tions.
I wash her shoulders, arms
legs thick like cauliflower stalks
beneath bedsheets
twisted and damp.
I hurry with washcloths warm
and limp because I do not
want to be alone with Death.
I wash between her legs, gently,
around the catheter hanging
yellow as a lizard's tongue
from withered folds

I wonder if she has ever been
truly touched there before.

The room is so blue,
an eerie, filtered azure.
Noise in the hall settles into sand.
Sister Ford sighs,
the kind a body takes
when faced with the inevitable.
I watch her chest like a sailor scans the sky
Please God, rise.
I thought Death would be definite,
certain like shattered glass
or the crack of thunder
but it is like melting. I stop
the water from the basin spills
out onto my shoes, the floor wet and slick.

They bring a bright yellow body bag
from the storeroom.
I help pack gauze
into her sacred untouched orifices,
fold her arms over her chest,
tie her small hands and feet
down for the convenience of the morgue.

Tethered to this earth by stones
and health that seem so safe,
I tighten the leather strap
feel another notch pull
around my own white-coated waist.

Ocean City, New Jersey

We walk along the beach, my father and I
Away from the carnival wheel spinning into the sky,
the fortune tellers, cotton candy wisps,
thirteen-year-old smokers crouching

down in the dunes.
We step over crushed glass and litter,
red tin lids of Mad Mac Chew
until the boardwalk is mute.
Behind us, our footprints pool with water

the waves, deep folds of obsidian
unroll on to the shore
like ribbons of black velvet.
My father picks up a few flat stones, skips
them across the tips of crested waves with a flick
of his wrist, arms thick and freckled.
The sun splits its golden yoke onto the sea

and we turn to go.
I don't see the stingray
buried beneath sand:
just two terrible eyes
pleading.
My toes edge

over its bizarre, flat body. I recoil,
shriek. But my father grasps its spiny tail
holds it upside-down
suspended
the ray's puckered mouth cinching shut
and small eyes blinking.
Even the waves are still. For a moment

my father, Solomon
bathed in pink sea light. He tosses the ray back

we watch it flex,
slip into the shifting greens

a thin, gray wafer
dissolving.

Unseen

When I was 10
we took apart the old T.V.
with a red-handled screwdriver, ball pen hammer
and some weird type of wrench

You set it on the counter
like a patient on an operating table
cracked the back off
a tangle of bright wires sprang forth
like Medusa's hair
wild and wound among thousands of tiny tubes
and flat green plates
stacked, studded with silver

I touched them
like braille
trying to understand

It took hours
to dissect our way down
to the impenetrable gray cube
at its base
the soul of the thing
where I was sure
the answers lived

I could not believe
what had been there all along
inside that broken, dusty box

Later, you brought home a microscope
and told me to look
And so, I did:

at a drop of my own blood
a strand of your hair

hamster fur
saliva
tobacco from your pipe
a dogwood leaf
dirt

The invisible, visible
with a half-turn of a dial

Now, you yourself are unseen
have been for a decade
I think of all that is there
that I cannot see
All that, which I know
you must long
to reveal

Sprinklers

July, and
cotton heat
clings, moist as a salamander's spotted back
I lick popsicles with my sister
on the coolness of the patio pavement
shirts off, freckles blooming

Sticky color
trails into crooks of elbows
dries there,
faint green
We are martians
with sunburned cheeks
and nubs for nipples

We drag the sprinkler
from the cavernous garage
dust it off, run our fingers
over the water-hole openings
pretend we are blind and they are braille
Mother yells through the screen door
for heaven's sake put some clothes on
but we stick out lime tongues
dance naked in the mist
that falls like gauze
on our bronzed backs

The sprinkler waving
curtains of rainbows
back and forth across our sky

Milton

sleeps, cradled in the curves
of the Susquehanna
pressed against her fall-shored skin
uneven sidewalks, stubborn weeds
push between the cracks
outside old row homes
that lean together
slouched and sagging
heads tilted inward
deep in thought

He wipes the dust
from chipped bifocals
sets them back into the two worn moon-grooves
along the bridge of his nose
and sighs
windchimes loose and lyrical
lift the wood-rotten porch

The autumn air remembers
back beyond the low-sunk fields
where corn husks rustle like starched silk
the way her blouse gaped
around the slope of her breasts
the grainy damp earth kissing
her back and thin
yellow hair drying
over summer-shoulders

strands of silky blond web
floating in and around
his mouth

Rape

I.   Necrosis

Lunch time with hoagies from WaWa
Everything was so normal, then
my parents rushed away.
Later, phrases through the door
only fourteen...party...sweet Jesus!...someone call...poor!

I ate tomatoes with mayonnaise. Refused to believe
because I knew you were infallible.

II.   Debridement

Tell all the newspapers! Print it on the front page!
Neatly after the weather, before the obituaries.
Each typeset letter safe
in its small catacomb home.
Damn these half-truths
parachutes with gaping holes

I told your secret
visceral and ugly to one friend
giddy with the small sick
glory of confession.

III.   Granulation

Yesterday you unfolded yards
and yards of black satin
wrapped yourself in the rich softness,
told me of the dress you'll make.

Even now, I walk in your wake.

Guilt, my anvil
when will you fall?

South

Mia's room

is still purple. Sassy Lilac at 50%, to be precise
We worked hard
to get the color right

I should re-paint
I say now
in a home that is too quiet
and too clean

As if two coats of Nantucket Breeze
or Summer Splash
could cover the pain
of falling in love
with someone else's daughter

After you left, I moved the bed
and found pieces of her—
a shiny, pink crystal, Dora's one blue shoe,
that hair tie
missing for months

I found pieces of me, too—
the voice that read Small Pig and the Slow Sloth,
hands that bandaged unicorn horns,
made elf's blood and witches' brew, combed for lice
and seashells

When you were at work
I washed her small, slippery back
gave apple slices
and good night kisses

No one warned me
how a child will ambush
the untethered heart

I can forgive almost everything
But not motherhood, amputated
in the driveway

July rain pouring down

bending the zinnias, their blamed heads
hanging heavy
in the storm

Nest

I.

You were drinking again
but still managed to monitor
the bluebird box

It was our second brood that year
the first had done so well
except the one fledgling that tried,
but died
we weren't sure why

I was away
and each day you checked
the four, pale perfect eggs

Then, one morning there was one less
I read blogs and books, it wasn't clear
We agree three will be okay
You fixed the baffle
to keep predators away

The next day the nest was down to two.

Then one.

And none.

I came home.

You were gone.

II.

In the scrubby margin
where yard meets forest
I find them

Four blue shells on the ground
pierced straight through

I pick one up, turn it over
in my palm

delicate and light as lace

How foolish to believe
that each day
what survived
would be enough

Wheat without grain,
flesh without form.

Packing Out

Late each night
the Colonel's son
watches the O Club clear out
and the whores with low-slung breasts
open their shutters and coo to green GIs
in palm frond voices

He crouches on the veranda's yellow sofa
—knees tucked to chin
white T-shirt stretched over legs—
chased there by nightmares of skeletons
who come to take away his friends

The leaves turn somersaults
above the paint-peeled porch
Thunder and soon
rain mists through the screens
a summer baptism that dews his arms
and wakes the skeletons

He hears them creak through the back door
tiny toe tarsals *clink, clink, clink*
on the kitchen tile
They poke sharp bones
against boxes
that line the hall
like a squatty brown train

He sits wide-eyed
the humid air pressing
down on his shoulders
like a hundred heavy hands
The Colonel and his wife
sleep through the skeletons
rising from the forest
rattling in their son's room

But he knew they would be here soon
these black-socketed beasts
who come to carry away
This Base

and These Friends

A gray wash settles over everything
a soft, snowy ash
that falls and sifts through the screens
and perfectly records
their steps

Weight

I.

Stretched out
on a borrowed settee
in afternoon light
warm and suspended
like the full, sweet swell of a cello

overdue to deliver
a thing fresh and new, of bone
and sinew
with labor borne of our past,
a bearing down of life

II.

This I know:
you are the buoy, the beacon
all light and safety
charting the only course
that has ever mattered

to a shoreline sculpted with dunes
where we can lie
in soft hills of sand
watch white-tipped waves,
the rough and wild waters
that marked us

III.

Perhaps there is comfort
in the pieces of the past
we hold to the light
the ones that reflect
back to us
an imperfect, prismed path

scatter small rainbows
at our feet

Borders

I long to push you

up the spiral stairwell
of Sainte-Chapelle
into the jeweled, shifting shadows
of stained glass

what I would give
to see your face
take in the light

aboard a houseboat
in the brackish backwaters of Kerala
fishing nets dipping and stretching
like the silhouette
of a giant praying mantis
feasting against a scarlet dusk

through the crooked labyrinth
of a Cairo souq
dusty and still
a thousand bright lanterns
swaying above the smell
of burning trash and sweet tobacco

But this map
with borders ragged, territory wild
cries for courage
red-fisted,
quick and sharp as silver

Patio 803

We shouldn't be here
but we are
both in the margin
and the vanguard
thrust

against the glass
behind which all
is out of reach
but clearly seen

bright, yet cruel
like sun off snow
that burns
and blinds

If you find a way
to break it
soundless
without shards

you must tell me
and press the answer
firmly
to my mouth

Father's Day

Our neighbor called the police
because it was 3 am
and the dogs were barking
relentless staccato
punctuating the frigid
February night

You let them out
but not back in
drunk on the couch
dulled by the singular effort
it takes to disappear

I drove home early
through the morning fog
to find two dogs dead
curled tight as knots on the back stoop
fur stiff-tipped with frost
scratch marks etched in the door
desperate grooves tinged with blood
their bodies now heavy
and cold

I touch my shoulders
remember my own yoke
and its weight
easily the weight of several lives

East

Epiphyte

This word I learn
walking below
bromeliads, cattleyas
a thousand rare orchids

reminds me of you

Twisted raw roots
exposed
like saphenous veins
catch second-hand rain
make food
out of air

You choose fragile beauty
each day
simply accept
what falls
through the forest
to nourish
your waiting roots

Alopecia

G1   new
beautiful, bright
globed heads
reveal hidden scars
unknown moles
stork bites, birthmarks

S   smooth like a polished doorknob
or rough with gray stubble
stray strands hang on
beg to stay
attached to a scalp
that let go weeks after chemo

G2   follicles fail, leave
a trace of you
on the chair, by the window
where you lean
toward waning winter light
the weak stem
of a pale and hopeful plant

M   panels of afternoon sun
shift above you
like haloes, elusive
uncertain
and just slightly
out of reach

The Old Artist and the Apprentice

They brought you here with weak lungs
and a strong heart
gave you a fern for your window
hid your cigarettes

I watch you breathe
through a tangle of soft tubes
show you my latest work
you smile, beg to go outside
for a smoke

You are a difficult subject
slippery like the colors that feed your grainy canvas
the way you sit on the uneven-legged stool
teetering, without a shirt
tufts of gray hair curling
in the cleft of your loose-nippled chest
one wrong movement from falling

I remember how you paint your women
gold, trapped in the pleated light of lanterns
your birch bark hands
speaking in sea-murmurs

I twist the rusted chains
of the porch swing
until my palms turn iron-brown
like the evening that falls
over the faces of the upturned hills

Explaining the Clover (again)

1.   I breathe bored
   peel my thighs
   from the orange vinyl kitchen chair

2.   You talk
   of rebellious South Street days
   sweaty drunk boys
   gecko-like against the cool pitted
   sideboard of Mario's Pizza Shop
   slurping sardines
   making bets

3.   I trace
   the tattoo
   raised by purple strained veins
   like a map

4.   A blue clover
   blooming
   along the cracked glazed skin
   of your ankle

West

Tucson

On the cusp of Sonoran dusk
the monsoon air hangs low
and heavy
I watch the sidewalks
freckle with rain

then spill madly
like ink
over gutters, turn
washes to rivers
flood streets and cemeteries

This sudden, angry water
with nowhere to go

releases the bitter
strange smell
of creosote from damp shrubs

that somehow grow
in caliche, that slice of desert stone
so unyielding
it has been known to break
all that try

Catharsis

I want—no,
I need, I *must*
shed this skin

as a snake sheds hers

Because all of this
has grown uncomfortably tight

Now, like cellophane
it gives way

easily, to a smooth
glistening, agile body
that bends and weaves
through the tall grass
faster and faster
before you realize:
>   *gone!*

Look quickly
at the onion-skin thin carcass left behind
how it holds my former shape—for just a moment
then collapses
like a folding ghost

Crumbles,
leaving
silver ash
in your hands

Clear Margins

i.

The scar on my stomach
looks like a paramecium

You observe this kindly,
ever the scientist
kissing my pale belly

And you are right:
it does.

Maybe I will make it into a tattoo, I say,
my legs scissored
over yours in decadent Sunday
afternoon laziness

Of what?
I don't know. Something with teeth,
not legs

ii.

How fitting
to find you
and then so soon
need to excise the bad,
make room for the healthy

like a lizard's sacrificial tail
that grows back stronger
or the first tender green shoots
pushing through
the charred soil
of a burnt forest

iii.

With you
I am like the sunflowers we planted
behind the bougainvillea
bright orange and fierce yellow, growing
giddy in the desert heat
towering impossibly high

above the faded stucco wall

Sun-drunk and sated,
ripe with warmth
from earth, from sky

Antaeus, 1994

I.

Rumor has it
Harrison Ford picks up hitchhikers along Route 20
offers them joints
rolled off the sweet Wyoming wind
and a night at his summer home in Jackson

I never met the actor
but a grizzled gun-collector
driving through to Salt Lake
in his Winnebago. I spent the day
watching geysers burst
golden and gray, tourists feeding
potato chips to yellow-haired marmots
Now they will find me with teeth unbrushed
underwear stained
a neat round hole through my forehead

Turns out he is strange, but safe
drops me at the gate, shrugs
you look so young

II.

300 bikers on their way to Sturgis
stop in for coffee
A table of four tips me 20 bucks
they cannot believe
I've never been on the back of a Harley
Wyoming has no helmet law, sweetheart

The road slate, we roll like marbles
into a kaleidoscope sky cut with serrated clouds
past bubbling paint pots
where hell's pained voices rise

A herd of buffalo dig
hooves into sagebrush, swing
shaggy brown bodies and bison bones
into unbelievable

unified motion. They run powerful
on cat-eye plains—
wide and yellow and mysterious

III.

A trio of spear-ribbed coyotes
dance on adobe dust
where the Popo Agie disappears
into the canyon

I remember the dead elk
along the blank highway
buzzards above, patient
for its gray pulseless meat

all at the mercy
of the raw
rough-linen wind

Poia Lake

Deep in the valley
edges soften
to dying shades of summer,
peaks are grandfathered
by late July snow.

Mountains suspend the sky
on two bitter points
like a giant tarp stretched above
a lake smooth as a satin cape
spinning with waterbugs.
They genuflect on thin-threaded legs
dance backwards
in crystal-beaded figure eights
to a silence
so tangible I can roll it in my palm
like the small colored stones
coaxed into smoothness
by the patient work of water.

I shed my clothes as a deer molts,
proud and with purpose.
Praise the cool water, the moist air.
Succumb to this moment
of summer baptism, spill sanctity
over and over my pale, thirsty skin.

Virginia **LeBaron** is faculty at the University of Virginia School of Nursing, where she conducts research on how to improve care for patients with cancer and teaches courses in human development and qualitative methods. She practiced as an oncology and palliative care nurse before entering academia, and her writing is shaped, in part, by these clinical experiences. This chapbook is her first published collection of poetry.

CPSIA information can be obtained
at www.ICGtesting.com
Printed in the USA
JSHW030028160321
12554JS00001B/26